Filling in the Map

EXPLORING INLAND AUSTRALIA

CAROLE WILKINSON

wild dog

First published in 2025 by

Melbourne, Australia
wdog.com.au

ISBN: 978-1-74203-655-7

10 9 8 7 6 5 4 3 2 1   25 26 27 28 29

Printed and bound in China by Everbest Printing Investment Limited

A catalogue record for this book is available from the National Library of Australia

FSC® is a non-profit international organisation established to promote the responsible management of the world's forests.

PICTURE CREDITS

End papers
From the *Book of sketches of Aboriginal life* by Tommy McRae

Images courtesy of National Library of Australia
p 1 Matthew Flinders, NLA, MAP T 1494; pp 2–3 John Arrowsmith, NLA, MAP T 115; p 7 Charles Grimes, NLA, MAP RM 711; p 14 John Arrowsmith, NLA, MAP T 115; p17 John Murray, C. Bradbury & W. Day, NLA, MAP RM 1836; p 18 Victoria, Education Department, MAP G8991.S12 1836; p 34 South Australia, Surveyor-General's Office, MAP RM 3510; pp 24–25 John Arrowsmith, NLA, MAP T 114; pp 26–27 John Arrowsmith, NLA, MAP RM 791; p 27 Aussie~mobs, Mobsby Collection, Fryer Library, Brisbane, 7294139582; pp 30–31 Victoria, Department of Crown Lands and Survey, NLA, MAP RM 2464; p 33 J. Macfarlane, PIC Drawer 5053 #S4579; p 34 South Australia, Surveyor-General's Office, NLA, MAP RM 3510; pp 36–37 Alfred Wernam Canning, NLA, MAP G9021.P25 1910; Front Cover Charles Grimes, NLA, MAP RM 711.

Images courtesy of State Library of New South Wales
p 4 Tommy McRae, Mitchell library, PXA 2129; p 6 James Anderson, Mitchell library, ML 411; p 8 Emile Ulm, SPF/1396; p 10 P1/797; p 13 George Edwards Peacock, Mitchell library, ML 144; p 19 Mitchell library, ML 24; p 21 Thomas Mitchell, Dixson Library, DG*D 30.

Images courtesy of State Library of Victoria
p 11 Victoria, Department of Crown Lands and Survey, MAPS 820.5 AT 1824-1825; p 38 Ludwig Becker, MS13360; Front Cover Ludwig Becker, MS13360.

Image courtesy of State Library of South Australia
p 32 Penman & Galbraith, B 11201.

Image courtesy of State Library of Western Australia
p 37 The Battye Library.

Images courtesy of the Art Gallery of South Australia
p 15 J. M. Crossland, 0.598; p 28 Nicholas Chevalier.

Image courtesy of History Trust of South Australia
p 23 GN03284.

Image courtesy of Queensland State Archives
p 26 ITM1623011.

Image courtesy of National Archives Catalogue, USA
p 35 Department of the Interior, Patent Office, 50926044.

Image courtesy of Adobe Stock
Front Cover AdobeStock_175639036.

Carole Wilkinson is an internationally award winning and best-selling author based in Melbourne. Her *Dragonkeeper* series won two CBCA Book of the Year awards and has recently been made into a movie. Her non-fiction titles include *Black Snake: The Daring of Ned Kelly*, *10 Pound Pom*, *Matthew Flinders: Adventures on Leaky Ships*, and *River to Bay*, which was shortlisted for the 2024 Victorian Community History Awards. *Filling in the Map* is a follow up to her 2020 book, *Putting Australia on the Map*.

Contents

Introduction

When the First Fleet arrived in Australia in 1788, Governor Arthur Phillip chose a sheltered cove as the site of Australia's first colony. Captain Cook had named it Port Jackson, but in 1788, Governor Phillip renamed the colony after the British Home Secretary, Lord Sydney.

Mariners from around the world had been visiting Australia for more than 200 years, but Sydney was its first permanent European settlement.

Australia's Aboriginal people had lived on the continent for more than 60,000 years. They consisted of more than 700 clans with 250 language groups. European settlers believed the land belonged to them, not the people who had lived on it for thousands of years. They felt entitled to take whatever land they wanted.

Aboriginal people were inquisitive about the newcomers and often offered help, but many fought to protect their Country when it became clear that Europeans had no respect for land, people or culture.

Matthew Flinders had accurately mapped Australia's coastline, but no physical map existed of inland Australia. For European settlers Australia was a 7.7 million km^2 mystery to solve.

Aboriginal people knew their Country in detail. A network of tracks across the continent, called Songlines, contained detailed knowledge of plants, animals and water sources. Aboriginal clans shared knowledge of Country through these Songlines, which use mythical, physical and astronomical landmarks as a guide as well as containing information on food, water, history and cultural law.

The Europeans used Aboriginal people for their precious knowledge of the land, usually without consent. Many of Australia's roads, highways and passes are the original tracks and Songlines of its Traditional Owners.

OPPOSITE: *Hunting possums and goannas*, circa 1885.

Crossing the Blue Mountains

Blaxland, Lawson and Wentworth 1813

The colony grew, spreading from Sydney to the Blue Mountains. With deep gorges and vertical sandstone cliffs, the mountain range seemed to be an impenetrable barrier to further exploration. The local Aboriginal clans, including the Gundungurra, Dharawal, Wiradjuri, Wanaruah, Darug and Darkinjung people, knew how to cross them, but they did not share their knowledge with the newcomers invading their Country.

At first the mountains were an advantage to the New South Wales government. The rugged landscape prevented the escape of convicts assigned to work for free settlers. But as Sydney's population increased, so did the need for more agricultural land. In May 1813, English settlers Gregory Blaxland and William Lawson, and Australian-born William Charles Wentworth set out from Emu Plains, west of Sydney, to find a way across the Blue Mountains.

ABOVE: *William Charles Wentworth 1872.*
OPPOSITE: A topographical plan of the settlements of New South Wales, 1799.

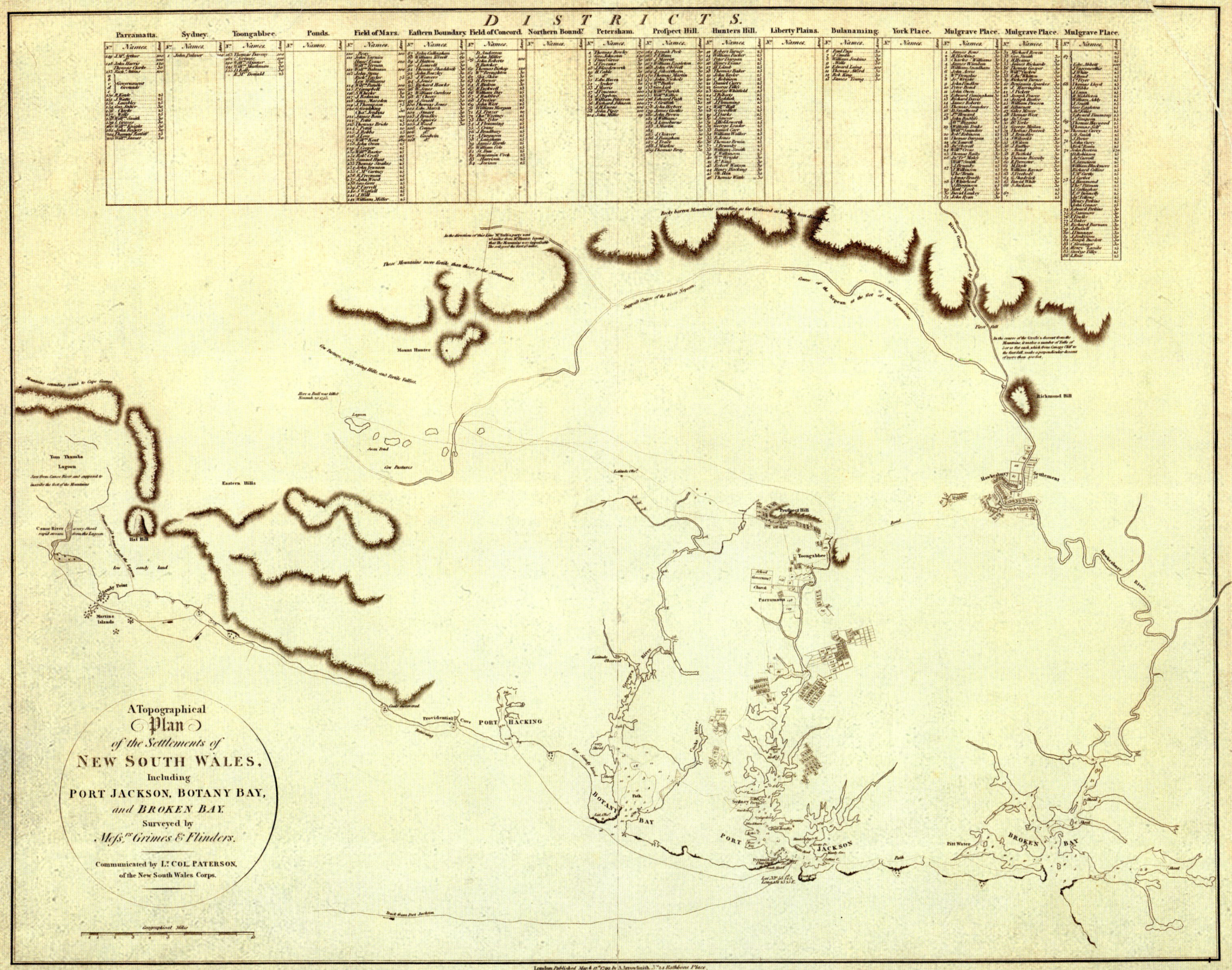
D I S T R I C T S.
Parramatta.
Sydney.
Toongabbee.
Ponds.
Field of Mars.
Eastern Boundary.
Field of Concord.
Northern Boundy.
Petersham.
Prospect Hill.
Hunters Hill.
Liberty Plains.
Bulanaming.
York Place.
Mulgrave Place.
Mulgrave Place.
Mulgrave Place.
Rocky barren Mountains extending as the Westward as has been discovered
Mount Hunter
Richmond Hill
Hawkesbury Settlement
Hawkesbury River
Tom Thumbs Lagoon
Eastern Hills
Hat Hill
Canoe River
Prospect Hill
Toongabbee
Parramatta
Church
PORT HACKING
BOTANY BAY
PORT JACKSON
BROKEN BAY
Pitt Water
A Topographical
Plan
of the Settlements of
NEW SOUTH WALES,
Including
PORT JACKSON, BOTANY BAY,
and BROKEN BAY.
Surveyed by
Mefs.rs Grimes & Flinders.
Communicated by Lt. COL. PATERSON,
of the New South Wales Corps.
Geographical Miles
London Published March 12th 1799 by A. Arrowsmith. No. 24 Rathbone Place.

Instead of trying to scale the cliffs or find a gorge through the mountains as previous explorers had done, they followed a ridge across the top from east to west. The ridge was only 20 m wide, covered in thick scrub, and had deep rocky gorges on either side. Each morning, the party left their packhorses behind and cut through the scrub on foot. They then retraced their steps and led the horses along the new path.

After three weeks, almost out of food, the party reached the edge of the mountains. A grassy plain stretched into the distance below them. It had taken 25 years, but Europeans had finally found a way across the mountains and discovered land suitable for agriculture. The men returned to Sydney with the good news.

George Evans, the colony's Assistant Surveyor, was the first European to make the full journey across the Blue Mountains and down to what is now called the Bathurst Plains. In 1815, Bathurst became Australia's first inland European settlement.

OPPOSITE: *The Blue Mountain pioneers at the summit of their expedition.*

A Fortunate Error

Hume and Hovell 1824

Australian-born Hamilton Hume began exploring New South Wales when he was 17. He had almost 10 years' experience as an explorer when Governor Brisbane appealed for someone to investigate the land from the south of Sydney to the Bass Strait coast. William Hovell, a retired English sea captain, joined Hume in his exploration. While Hovell had little bush experience, he knew how to navigate by the stars. When Governor Brisbane lost interest in the project, Hume and Hovell decided to fund the expedition themselves, taking six convict servants with them.

Hume and Hovell's destination was Western Port, a bay in what is now Victoria. The party had to cross 10 rivers, including the flooded Murrumbidgee and an even larger river which they named the Hume. Crossing rivers with carts packed with stores took ingenuity. They converted one cart into a boat and hauled it across the waterways. As well as rivers, the men negotiated

ABOVE: *Studio portrait of Hamilton Hume*, circa 1869.
OPPOSITE: *Map showing track of Hume and Hovell across Victoria.*

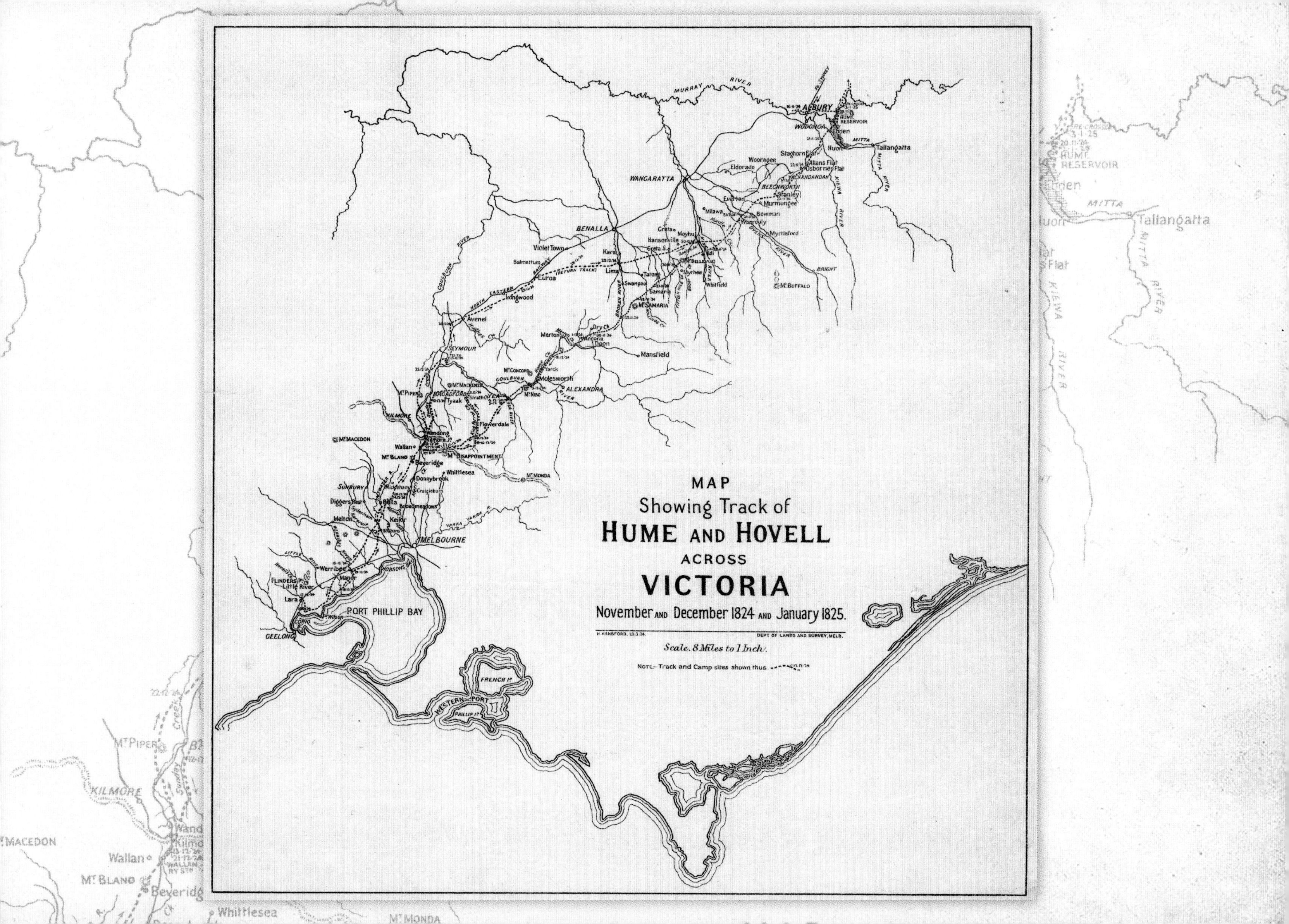
MAP
Showing Track of
HUME AND HOVELL
ACROSS
VICTORIA
November AND December 1824 AND January 1825.
H. HANSFORD, 20.3.24.
DEPT OF LANDS AND SURVEY, MELB.
Scale. 8 Miles to 1 Inch.
NOTE.– Track and Camp sites shown thus
MURRAY RIVER
ALBURY
WODONGA
HUME RESERVOIR
Ebden
Huon
MITTA
Tallangatta
MITTA RIVER
WANGARATTA
Eldorado
Wooragee
Staghorn Flat
Allans Flat
Osbornes Flat
YACKANDANDAH
BEECHWORTH
Stanley
Murmungee
Everton
Milawa
Bowman
Myrtleford
KIEWA RIVER
BRIGHT
BENALLA
Violet Town
Balmattum
Euroa
Longwood
Karn
Lima
Moyhu
Hansonville
Greta
Tarong
Swanpool
Samaria
Myrhee
Whitfield
Mt BUFFALO
Mt SAMARIA
BROKEN RIVER
GOULBURN RIVER
NORTH EASTERN RAILWAY
(RETURN TRACK)
Avenel
SEYMOUR
Merton
Dry Ck
Doon
Mansfield
Mt CONCORD
Yarck
Molesworth
ALEXANDRA
Mt NIRO
YEA
GOULBURN
Mt PIPER
BROADFORD
Mt MACKENZIE
Tyaak
Strath
Flowerdale
KILMORE
Mt MACEDON
Wandong
Kilmore Jn
Wallan
Mt BLAND
Mt DISAPPOINTMENT
Beveridge
Whittlesea
Mt MONDA
SUNBURY
Diggers Rest
Mickleham
Donnybrook
Craigieburn
Bulla
Broadmeadows
Melton
Keilor
YARRA YARRA R.
MELBOURNE
HOBSONS BAY
Werribee
FLINDERS Pk
Little River
Manor
Lara
Wilson
CORIO
PORT PHILLIP BAY
GEELONG
FRENCH Id
WESTERN PORT
PHILLIP Id

mountain ranges and had to leave their carts behind.

Hume and Hovel met Aboriginal clans during their journey. Hume had encountered Aboriginal people in his early explorations in New South Wales and was able to communicate with them despite not understanding their language.

After 11 weeks, the party arrived at what they thought was Western Port. However, Hovell had miscalculated the longitude and they were actually in Corio Bay, Port Phillip. It was a fortunate error because the land surrounding Corio Bay was, according to Hovell, "Delightful ... with every possible advantage attached to it." This is where the town of Geelong was founded.

Thirty years after their expedition, Hume and Hovell had a quarrel. Hume believed Hovell was presenting himself as the leader of their expedition and published a 79-page pamphlet listing his complaints about his fellow explorer. Hume claimed the expedition was his idea, and had succeeded because of his leadership. He wanted his name first whenever they were mentioned together.

Hume need not have worried. The pair is usually remembered as "Hume and Hovell".

OPPOSITE: *The South Australian Alps as first seen by Messrs. Hovell and Hume on the 8th November 1824.*

Note.— Mr Arrowsmith has prepared a detailed Map of Captn Sturt's late Routes into the Interior, in 2 Sheets, which may be had in a cover — Price 7^s

Sketch Map of CAPTAIN STURT'S Tracks & Discoveries, on his Various Expeditions into SOUTH EASTERN & CENTRAL AUSTRALIA.

SOUTH AUSTRALIA

NEW SOUTH WALES

AUSTRALIA FELIX

GIPPS LAND

Note

Captn Sturt's Route 1844–5 Coloured .... Red

Rivers discovered & traced by Captn Sturt ..... Blue

Rivers traced by Captn Sturt, subsequent to their discovery by others .... Orange

English Miles. 0 50 100 200

London, T. & W. Boone 1849.

J. Arrowsmith.

The Mysterious Rivers of NSW

Sturt 1828, 1829, 1844

Born in India to English parents, Charles Napier Sturt arrived in Australia in 1827. Early explorers had expected the rivers of New South Wales to flow out to sea. They were surprised to find they instead flowed west and north-west. Sturt thought that the rivers must flow into a great inland sea.

In 1828, Governor Darling approved Sturt's exploration of the Macquarie River area. The expedition departed from the Wellington Valley, north-west of Sydney, in early November and later that month Hamilton Hume joined Sturt as his first assistant.

When returning to the Wellington Valley in April 1829, the party discovered a west-flowing river and named it the Darling.

The following year, Sturt's second expedition followed the Lachlan and the Murrumbidgee rivers. Sturt rowed a whaleboat down the Murrumbidgee until he reached a wide river, which he named the Murray. This was the same river

ABOVE: Portrait of Captain Charles Sturt, 1853.
OPPOSITE: *Sketch map of Captain Sturt's tracks & discoveries on his various expeditions into south eastern central Australia.*

that Hume and Hovell had called the Hume.

Sturt solved the mystery of the west and north-west-flowing rivers, discovering that most of them eventually flowed into the Murray. He continued to follow the Murray, which, after steadily heading north-west, suddenly turned south. Sturt followed it to a lake, which he named Lake Alexandrina. Over the sand hills he discovered a narrow channel of water which emptied into the Indian Ocean. The mighty Murray River ended as a stream too small for shipping. After this disappointment, Sturt and his party rowed almost 1500 km home – against the current.

Fifteen years later, Sturt had moved to Adelaide. Once more he set out in search of a great inland sea. This time he travelled north from Adelaide. With searing summer heat and no rain, Sturt decided to stop at a place with permanent water. He named it Depot Glen. The heat was unbearable, so Sturt organised his men to dig an underground shelter where they would wait for rain. They waited almost seven months.

Sturt led his expedition north-west to what he thought was the centre of the continent. Instead of a great inland sea, he found the Stony Desert and the Simpson Desert.

OPPOSITE: Country near the mouth of the River Murray Australia, 1833.

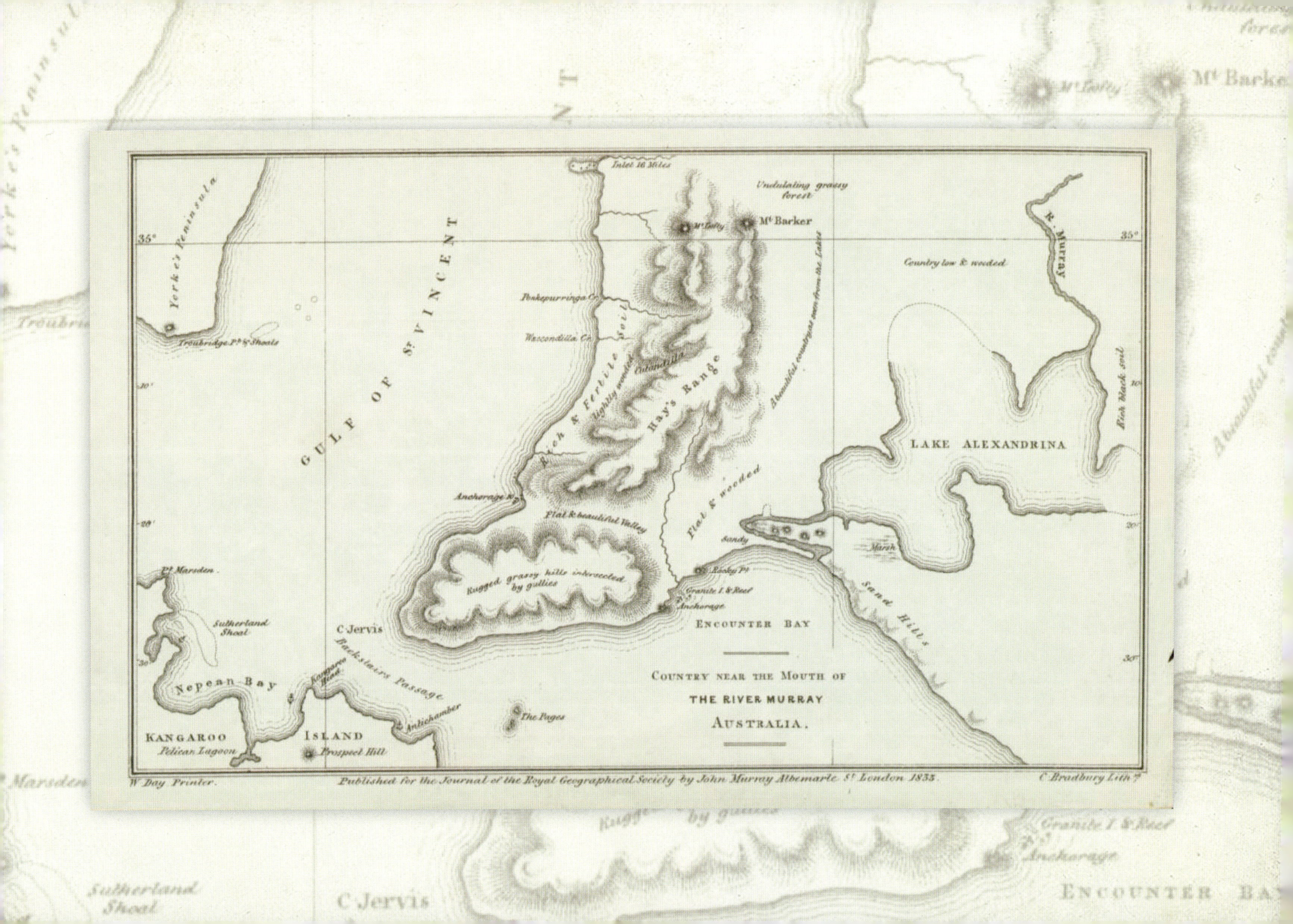

COUNTRY NEAR THE MOUTH OF
THE RIVER MURRAY
AUSTRALIA.

Inlet 16 Miles
Undulating grassy forest
Mt Lofty
Mt Barker
35°
Yorke's Peninsula
GULF OF St VINCENT
Country low & wooded
R. Murray
Troubridge Pt & Shoals
Ponkepurringa Cr.
Wacondilla Cr.
Rich & Fertile Soil
Lightly wooded
Cuandilla
Hay's Range
A beautiful country as seen from the Lakes
Rich black soil
LAKE ALEXANDRINA
Anchorage
Flat & beautiful Valley
Flat & wooded
Sandy
Marsh
Rocky Pt
Rugged grassy hills intersected by gullies
Granite I. & Reef
Anchorage
Pt Marsden
Sutherland Shoal
C. Jervis
ENCOUNTER BAY
Sand Hills
Backstairs Passage
Nepean Bay
Kangaroo Head
Antichamber
The Pages
KANGAROO
ISLAND
Pelican Lagoon
Prospect Hill

W. Day Printer. Published for the Journal of the Royal Geographical Society by John Murray Albemarle St London 1835. C. Bradbury Lith.

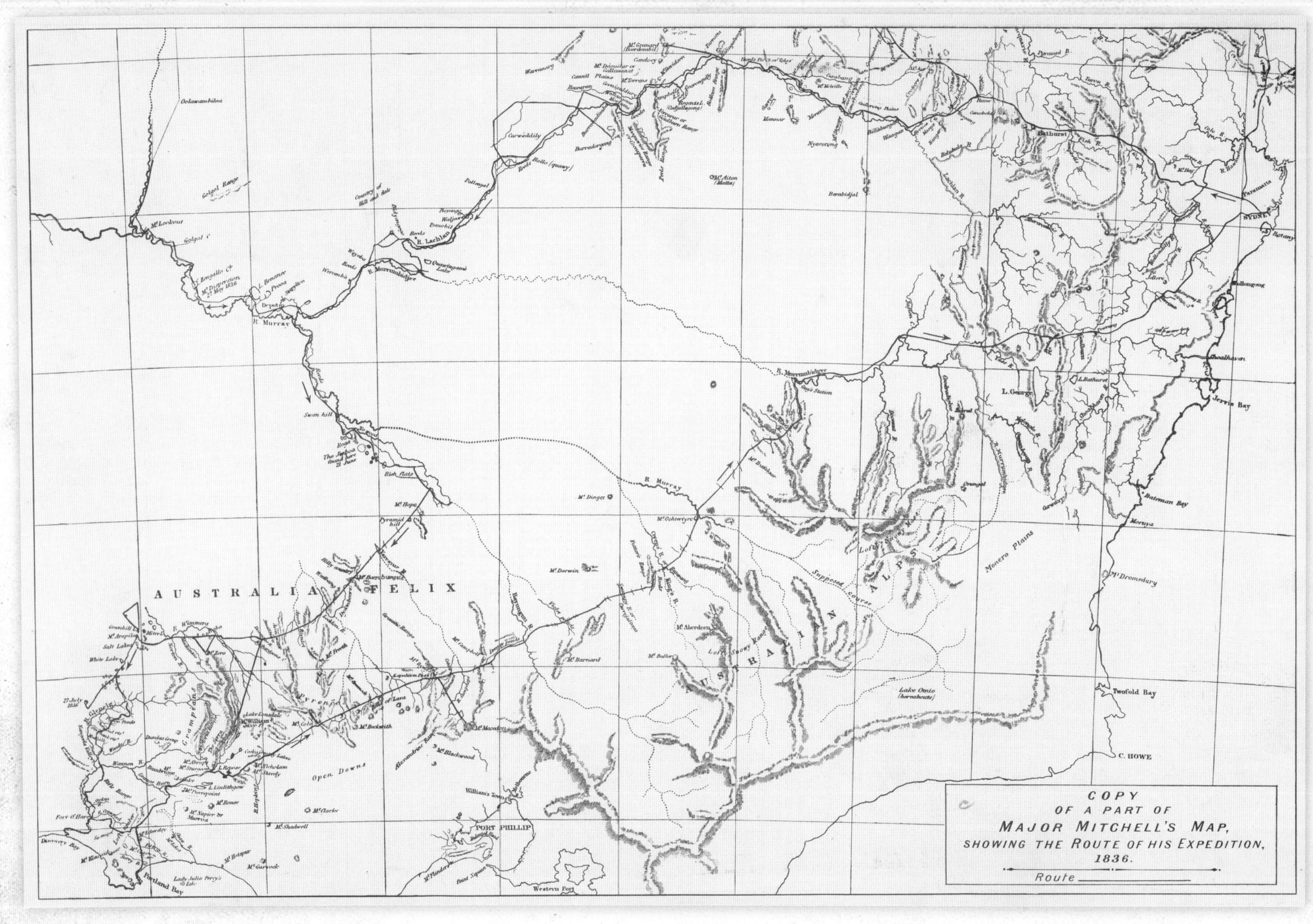
COPY
OF A PART OF
MAJOR MITCHELL'S MAP,
SHOWING THE ROUTE OF HIS EXPEDITION,
1836.
Route
AUSTRALIA FELIX
AUSTRALIAN ALPS
SYDNEY
Paramatta
Botany
Wollongong
Shoalhaven
Jervis Bay
Bateman Bay
Moruya
Mt. Dromedary
Twofold Bay
C. HOWE
Monero Plains
Lake Omio (hereabouts)
PORT PHILLIP
Western Port
Point Nepean
Portland Bay
Lady Julia Percy's Isle
Discovery Bay
Bathurst
L. George
L. Bathurst
R. Murrumbidgee
R. Murray
R. Lachlan
R. Wimmera
R. Glenelg
Grampians
Pyrenees
Open Downs
Mt. Macedon
Mt. Blackwood
Mt. Cole
Mt. Beckwith
Mt. William
Mt. Arapiles
Salt Lakes
White Lake
Mt. Hope
Pyramid hill
Swan hill
Mt. Lookout
Mt. Dispersion 1st May 1836
Depot
Mt. Dingee
Mt. Darwin
Mt. Aberdeen
Mt. Barnard
Mt. Aiton (Matta)
Supposed course
27 July 1836
William's Town
Mt. Napier or Murroa
Mt. Rouse
Mt. Clarke
Mt. Shadwell
Mt. Eccles
Mt. Kincaid
Fort O'Hare
Mt. Flinders
Alexandrine Range
Mt. Gambier
Mt. Bowen
Gundagai
Yass R.
Lachlan R.
Mt. Granard
Golgol Range
Oolawambiloa

The Disobedient Surveyor-General

Mitchell 1831, 1835, 1836

Thomas Livingstone Mitchell was a Scot who arrived in New South Wales in 1827. The following year he was appointed Surveyor-General. Mitchell led several major expeditions into the interior of eastern Australia during his time as Surveyor-General.

In 1831, an escaped convict claimed to have knowledge of a large river that Aboriginal people called Kindur. In November 1831, Mitchell set off with two surveyors and 15 convicts but found no trace of the river. During the expedition, Aboriginal warriors killed two members of Mitchell's party.

In 1835, Governor Darling sent Mitchell to discover where the Darling and Murray Rivers met. Mitchell charted the Bogan and Darling rivers, but did not go as far as the Murray.

The following year, Governor Bourke instructed Mitchell to find out whether the Darling flowed into the sea or into the Murray. Mitchell reached the junction of the Darling

OPPOSITE: *Copy of part of Major Mitchell's map, showing the route of his expedition, 1836.*
ABOVE: *Portrait of Sir Thomas Livingstone Mitchell*, circa 1835.

and the Murray, but then decided to travel south-west. In what is now Victoria, he discovered lush grasslands, excellent for farming, which he named "Australia Felix" – Latin for "Lucky Australia".

Mitchell often used Aboriginal place names in his writing, but when Aboriginal people tried to defend their Country, he called them "treacherous savages".

On his third expedition, Mitchell and his party discovered Aboriginal men armed with spears were following them. Without making contact or attempting to negotiate, Mitchell decided they must be members of the Barkindji people who had killed men on his first expedition. One of Mitchell's party fired his gun at the men and others followed his example. At least seven and up to 30 Aboriginal men were killed and others wounded in what became known as the Mount Dispersion Massacre.

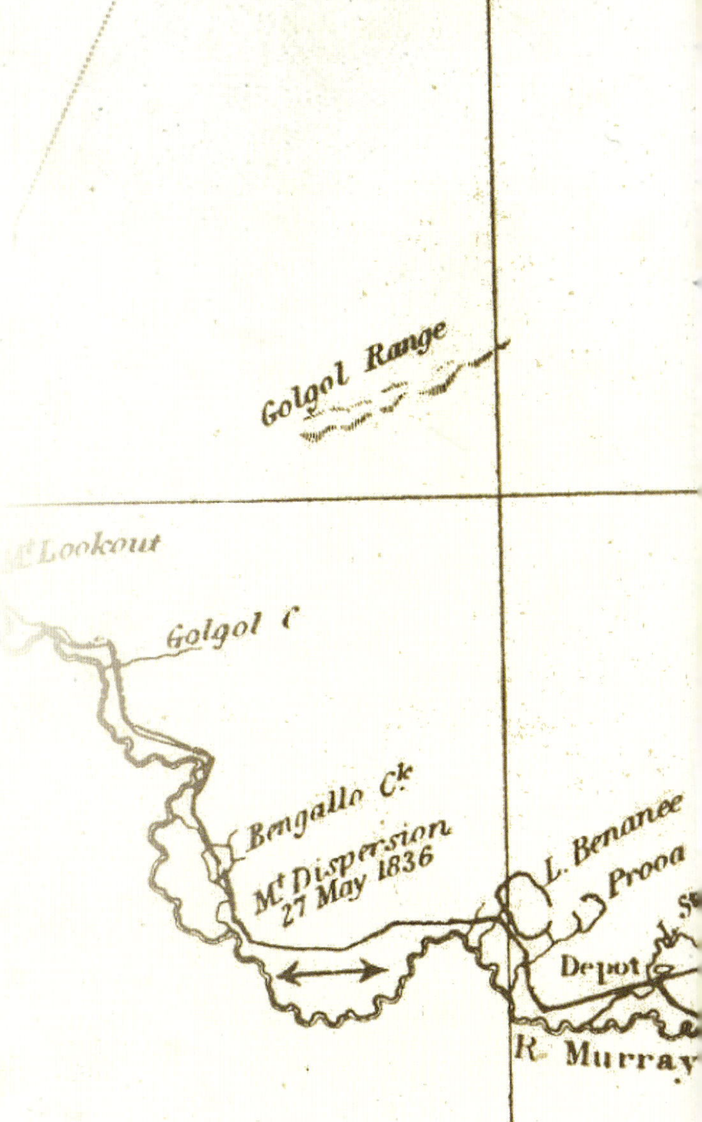

TURANDUREY

TURANDUREY – A WIRADJURI WOMAN, WHOSE HUSBAND had recently died – was one of Mitchell's Aboriginal guides. She had a four-year-old daughter, named Ballandella. It was unusual for females to be guides, but Turandurey proved to be a good interpreter. She helped Mitchell find water, food and good places to camp.

When Turandurey wanted to return to her people, she left Ballandella in Mitchell's care. Mitchell treated the girl as an experiment to see whether an Aboriginal child could be educated. Ballandella learned to read well.

LEFT: *Turandurey and Ballandella*, by Thomas Mitchell

The Head of the Bight

Eyre 1839, 1840

Englishman Edward John Eyre was 17 when he arrived in Australia in 1833. By the time he was 22, he had earned enough money to buy 1000 sheep and 600 cattle, which he drove from New South Wales to Port Phillip. Eyre also drove stock to South Australia.

With the profit from selling his stock, Eyre organised an expedition to explore inland Australia. In 1839, he travelled north of Adelaide, looking for good farming land. Eyre also searched for an inland sea, but like Sturt, found only desert.

Eyre wanted to be the first European to reach the head of the Great Australian Bight. In 1840 – at the age of 25 – he set out west with freed convict John Baxter, a Noongar man named Wylie, and two Aboriginal boys named Yarry and Joey. It took three attempts for them to reach the Head of the Bight.

The small party continued travelling west around the Bight. It was winter and cold at night. They were also running out of food and water, and Yarry and Joey did not want to continue. One night, while on watch, Eyre heard a gun being fired. He found Baxter dying of a gunshot wound, and no sign of the Aboriginal boys. They had gone, taking food, water and guns.

Eyre and Wylie continued west for more than a month. They dug holes in sand dunes to find water, and had to eat one of their horses. Just when it seemed they would die of thirst and hunger, Eyre and Wylie came upon a French whaling ship — the Mississippi — anchored in Thistle Cove. Taken aboard, Eyre and Wylie rested and ate well for 12 days. With fresh supplies and clothing, they continued on foot and reached King George Sound on 7 July 1841, completing a 3000 km journey. This was Wylie's Country and he was warmly welcomed home.

RIGHT: Etching of John Eyre and Wylie when first sighting a ship.

Eyre was one of the rare Europeans who understood how much settlement had disrupted Aboriginal peoples' lives. He believed they deserved compensation for the land and food sources settlers had taken from them. Eyre's journal included a section called *An Account of the Manners and Customs of the Aborigines and the State of their Relations with Europeans.*

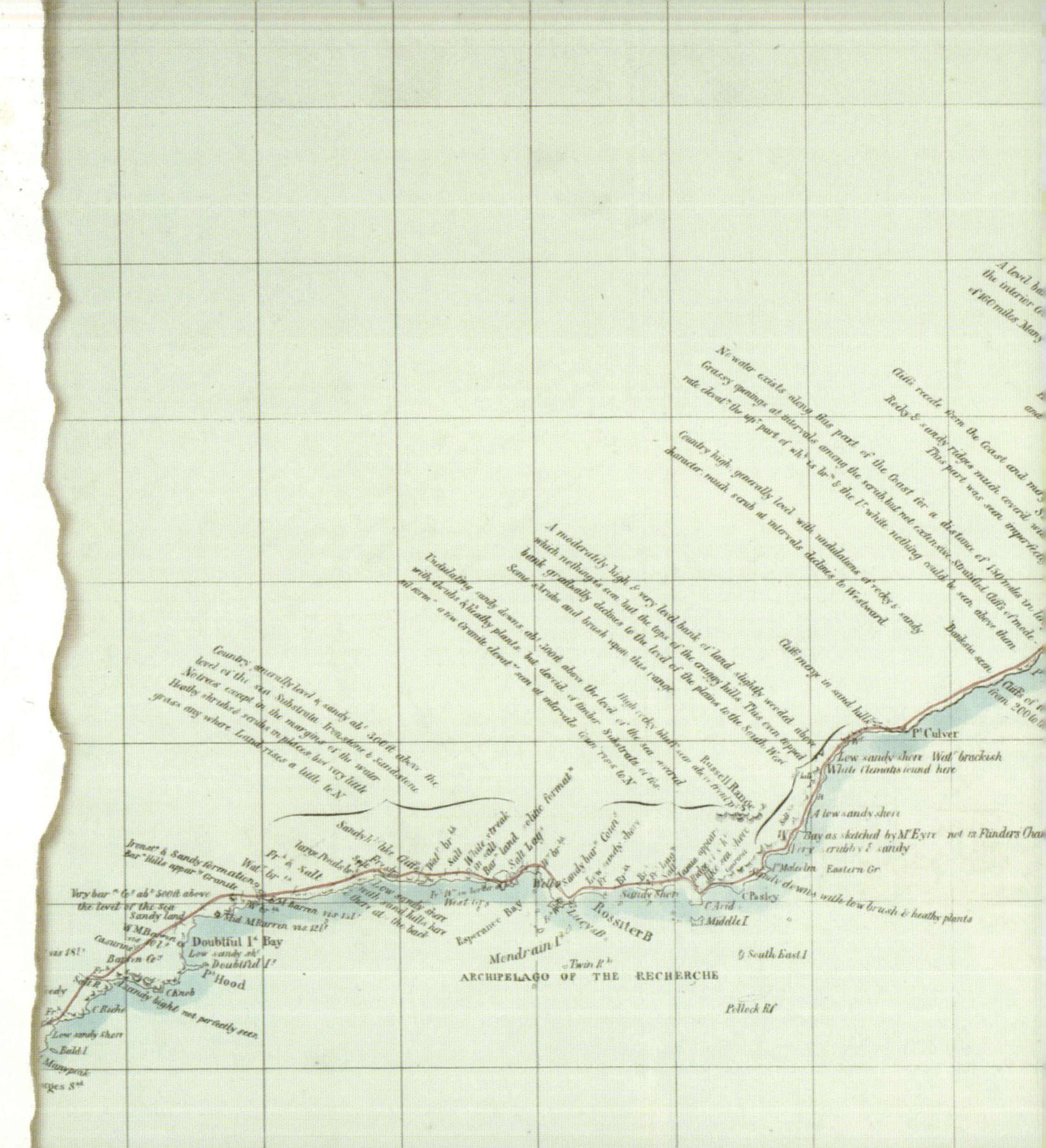

RIGHT: Map of the southern coast of Australia from Encounter Bay to King George's Sound showing Eyre's tracks.

A The Country betw.n the L & the hills appears to consist entirely of very low barren stony plains, washed smooth and even by the action of water, and in many places covered with salsolaceous plants, but otherwise destitute of vegetation and totally without water. These plains are intersected in many places by fragments of steep sided table land, varying in elevation from 50 ft to 300 ft & composed almost wholly of white
There is no timber of any kind, & but very few shrubs or bushes.
B The shore of the L is bounded by a steep sandy ridge, covered with salsola & small shrubs.
No grass nor fresh water
MAP
of the
SOUTHERN COAST OF AUSTRALIA,
FROM ENCOUNTER BAY TO KING GEORGE'S SOUND;
SHEWING M.r EYRE's TRACK IN THE YEARS 1839, 1840 & 41
in his attempt to penetrate into the interior.
Horse track
Dray d.o
HEAD OF THE GR.T AUSTRALIAN BIGHT
Gawler Range 2000 ft
Nuyt's Archipelago
Fowlers B
Streaky B
Anxious B
Investigators Gr
Coffins B
Port Lincoln
Sleaford B
SPENCERS GULF
Yorke's Peninsula
INVESTIGATOR STR
M.t Sturt
Cliffs of fossil formation from 400 to 600 ft and bluff into the Sea
Party obliged to send back for water
Scrubby bet.n the Cliffs & the shore
There appears to be W.r in middle of the Lake
M.t Eyres farthest N
Salt w.r in Channel
Middleback R
Harvey B
Peak

Lost

Leichhardt 1844, 1848

When German Friedrich Wilhelm Ludwig Leichhardt arrived in Sydney in 1842, he dreamed of becoming a famous explorer. He hoped to join an expedition from Sydney to Australia's northern coast, but when Governor Gipps would not fund the journey, Leichhardt raised the money himself.

In 1844, Leichhardt and nine other men embarked on an expedition from the northern edge of Queensland's Darling Downs. The team included an ornithologist and a botanist, but no one with bushcraft experience.

During the journey, Aboriginal warriors attacked the party and speared one of Leichhardt's men, John Gilbert, through the heart. This could have been because Leichhardt had taken a large amount of water lily seeds that the Aboriginal men had collected to eat.

Food supplies were running low, so Leichhardt and his men hunted kangaroo and emu to add to their menu. On Christmas Day, as a special treat, the men ate stewed cockatoos and suet pudding.

ABOVE: Profile of the German explorer Frederich Wilhelm Ludwig Leichhardt.
OPPOSITE: Detail from Leichhardt's tree on Marmadilla Station near Springsure, Queensland 1907.
BACKGROUND: Leichhardt's route from Moreton Bay to Port Essington, 1847.

After an exhausting journey of more than 14 months and 4800 km, Leichhardt and his men reached Port Essington on the northern coast. They had been presumed dead. They sailed to Sydney, where they were welcomed as heroes.

Leichhardt had achieved his goal of becoming a famous explorer, but he was not satisfied. He wanted to cross the country from east to west, expecting it would take them at least two years to reach the Swan River in Western Australia. He made his first attempt in 1846, but the expedition turned back after six months when they succumbed to sickness, possibly dengue fever.

Two years later, Leichhardt was ready to try again. His party of seven men, seven horses, 20 mules and 50 bullocks set out from the Darling Downs in April 1848. They were never seen again.

Search parties found trees carved with the letter "L" and a small brass plate with Leichhardt's name on it. But the remains of the explorer, his men and all his animals were never found. There are theories — the men starved, they drowned, Aboriginals killed them — but the true fate of Leichhardt's expedition remains a mystery.

Race to Disaster

Burke and Wills 1860

By 1860, the discovery of gold had made Victoria a wealthy colony. It seemed only right that a Victorian expedition should be the first to cross the continent from south to north. Robert O'Hara Burke, a former Irish policeman, was serving as a Police Superintendent in regional Victoria when he was selected by committee to lead the expedition. He could speak French, Italian and German but a newspaper reported that "he could not tell the north from the south in broad daylight, and the Southern Cross as a guide was a never-ending puzzle to him".

William John Wills was appointed Burke's third-in-command. Wills had arrived in Australia from England when he was 18. He worked on a sheep station before moving to Melbourne to work at the Observatory, where he learned to navigate by the stars.

Given a huge budget of £9000 (around $1,000,000 today), Burke equipped the expedition with 19 men, 23 horses and 26 camels. Six wagons were loaded with food for two years, as well as tonnes of equipment, including an oak table where Burke would write his journal, and a gong to call the men to meals. Burke also ordered 18 kg of pepper and 227 L of rum to revive the camels if they became tired.

The expedition left Melbourne in August 1860, but three wagons broke down before they reached the first night's stop at Essendon – only 10 km away.

OPPOSITE: *Memorandum of the Start of the Exploring Expedition, 1860.*

Burke was not a good leader. By the time the expedition reached Menindee, a small town in far west NSW, 15 members had resigned or been fired. Eight new members were hired and Wills was promoted to second-in-command.

Burke decided to make a depot at Menindee and to lead a small party to Cooper Creek. He left the wagons in charge of a man called Brahe.

Arriving at Cooper Creek, they were still less than halfway to their destination. With men and horses already weak from lack of food and water, Burke again divided his party. He knew his rival Stuart was also heading to the northern coast and was determined to beat him.

Burke, Wills and two others – John King and Charlie Gray – continued towards the Gulf of Carpentaria with supplies for three months.

After crossing the Stony Desert, Burke and Wills continued to the Gulf of Carpentaria alone. On about 11 February 1861, exhausted after struggling through the muddy mangrove swamps, and convinced they were close to the sea, the party began the return journey. Gray died on the trek back to Cooper Creek.

Meanwhile, Brahe waited more than four months for the explorers' return, but left just hours before they arrived. Brahe carved instructions into a tree, directing the men to where he'd buried the supplies. This tree, known as the Dig Tree, still stands. Burke, Wills and King found the cache, which had enough food for a month. Instead of following Brahe back to Menindee, they headed south-west to Mount Hopeless in South Australia.

After the party's two remaining camels died, the Yandruwandha people supplied them with fish and cakes made from the seeds of the nardoo plant. Burke accepted the gifts but did not like taking charity from people he saw as inferior. He ordered King to shoot over the Aboriginals' heads the next time they approached. Unsurprisingly, the gifts of food stopped.

Burke and Wills thought they could make their own nardoo cakes but did not know that the seeds had to be soaked first to extract an enzyme which destroys Vitamin B1, making it poisonous. Both men died, probably of the disease beriberi. King sought help from the Yandruwandha people, who cared for him until a rescue party arrived.

On 21 January 1863, thousands of people lined the streets of Melbourne to pay tribute as the remains of Burke and Wills were taken to the Melbourne Cemetery.

BACKGROUND: Map of Burke and Wills' route from Cooper Creek to Carpentaria.

A Wire Across Australia

Stuart 1858, 1859, 1860, 1862

John McDouall Stuart arrived from Scotland in 1839, and settled in South Australia. Stuart worked in the government's survey department and took part in Charles Sturt's 1844 expedition, an experience which inspired him to become an explorer.

In 1858, Stuart set out on his first expedition. With two men, he travelled for three months in search of good grazing land north of Adelaide. His only navigational equipment was a pocket compass and a watch. In 1859, with better equipment, Stuart led two expeditions and located springs fed by water from the Great Artesian Basin.

On his fourth expedition, Stuart discovered a mountain peak which he named Central Mount Sturt (later renamed Central Mount Stuart). Stuart thought the mountain was at the centre of Australia, but he was 400 km off the mark. He planted a flag, built a cairn of stones and made a speech about

LEFT: John McDouall Stuart, Esquire.
OPPOSITE: *John McDouall Stuart planting the Union Jack on Central Mount Stuart, 1860.*

J. Macfarlane

ADELAIDE AND PORT DARWIN

TELEGRAPH LINE

how British settlement would benefit Aboriginal people.

Stuart's next goal was to cross Australia from south to north. The newly invented telegraph had arrived in northern Australia from England and a telegraph line was needed between northern and southern Australia. The South Australian Government offered a £2000 reward to the first explorer to find a suitable route for a telegraph line between Adelaide and Port Essington.

Stuart made good progress on his first attempt, but suffered from scurvy and had to abandon the expedition. After several more failed attempts, he finally reached the northern coast. He stood on the beach, east of present-day Darwin on 24 July 1862, after a journey of nine months. On his return to Adelaide, Stuart was so sick from scurvy he had to be carried the last 640 km on a stretcher hung between two horses.

On the same day that Burke and Wills were buried in Melbourne, thousands of people lined Adelaide's streets to cheer the arrival of their hero, Stuart.

Burke and Wills might have been the first to cross the continent from south to north, but Stuart's route proved the most useful. In 1871, construction of a telegraph line began along Stuart's track. The Stuart Highway, built in the 1940s, also follows the route of Stuart's sixth expedition.

BACKGROUND: *Plan shewing the Adelaide and Port Darwin telegraph line.*

The Telegraph

American Samuel Morse was one of the main contributors to the invention of the telegraph in 1835. The telegraph required just one wire which could travel under the sea and over land. An operator tapped out a message using Morse Code.

By 1866, the telegraph connected America, Europe and India.

The construction of the telegraph line from Adelaide to Port Essington took two years. It consisted of 4600 km of galvanised wire strung between 36,000 iron poles. Operators at repeater stations every 200 to 300 km wrote down the signal and retransmitted it to the next station.

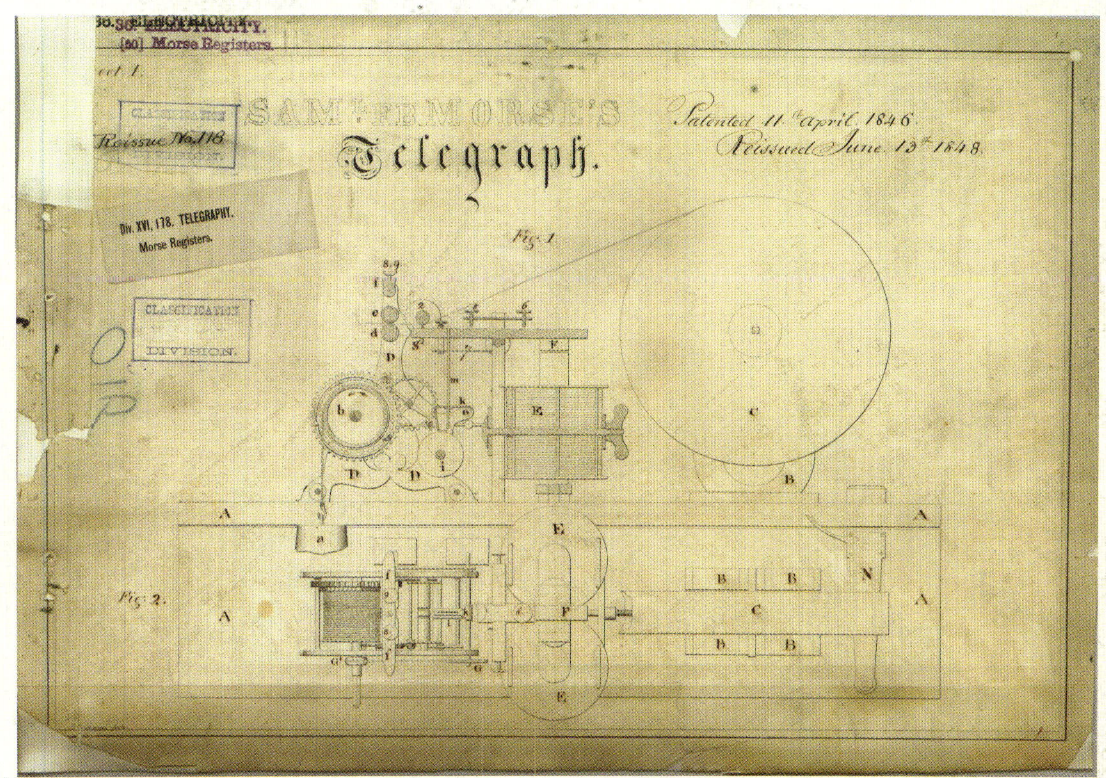

A single wire between Port Essington and Adelaide now connected Australia to the world. News no longer took months to arrive by ship. Instead, it was transmitted in hours.

ABOVE RIGHT: Patent for Samuel Morse's Telegraph, 1846.

No Justice

Canning 1906

Melbourne-born Alfred Wernam Canning spent four years in Western Australia surveying the route for the 1900 km No.1 Fence, known as the Rabbit Proof Fence, which was meant to keep rabbits from eastern states out of WA.

Western Australia's population increased rapidly following the discovery of gold in the late 1890s. With beef in short supply at the goldfields, cattle station owners were keen to supply live cattle to the miners without passing through areas infested with cattle ticks.

In 1906, the Western Australian Government came up with the idea of a stock route from the Kimberley district to the goldfields, with wells every 25 km to provide water. Canning, with his experience in surveying unsettled areas, got the job of creating that route.

Canning's expedition included seven experienced men, horses and 23 camels to carry equipment, food and drums of water. He needed the help of Martu and Wangkatjungka men to lead the expedition to reliable water sources.

Back in Perth, when Canning reported that he had found a route with 52 wells and reasonable grass, he received a standing ovation in Parliament.

Not everyone thought Canning was a hero. The expedition's cook accused him of mistreating the Aboriginal guides. He said they did not join the expedition freely and were shackled together with neck chains at night to prevent escape.

Canning gave them salt water to drink, so that they would be forced to lead him to fresh water or die of thirst.

A Royal Commission into the treatment of the Aboriginal men found Canning not guilty, even though he admitted to taking neck chains and handcuffs on the expedition.

Canning was chosen to lead a second expedition, to make permanent, deep wells and provide water troughs for cattle. This time he took 100 tonnes of boring tools. Some of the new wells were very deep with steep sides, which made it difficult and dangerous for Aboriginal people to access the water in what had once been their own wells.

RIGHT: Alfred Wernam Canning.
BACKGROUND: Wiluna-Kimberley stock route.
OVERLEAF: *First camp from Duroadoo.*

Explorers' Food

Expeditions could last weeks, months or sometimes more than a year. As well as equipment, explorers had to carry all the food they would need. With no eskies or car fridges, they could only take food that would not spoil.

Explorers often found themselves on reduced rations as their journey progressed.

Damper — made with flour, and, if the travellers were lucky, salt — was cooked on campfires. Some expeditions took a small flock of sheep so they could have fresh meat. Others relied on their hunting skills and ate kangaroo, emu, duck, fish, yabbies and other wild animals. But not all explorers were good hunters. Many were forced to eat their pack animals — horses, bullocks and camels — as their supplies dwindled.

These are the weekly rations, per person, on one of Sturt's expeditions:

10 lbs (4.5 kg) of flour
2 lbs (1 kg) of sugar
¼ lb (100 g) of tea
¼ lb (100 g) tobacco
2 oz (50 g) of soap

Glossary

£: The symbol for the pound, the currency in Great Britain and early Australia.

BERIBERI: A disease caused by lack of Vitamin B1. It affects the heart, or the nervous system, and can cause death.

BOTANIST: Someone who studies plants.

DAMPER: Bread made with flour and water, cooked in campfire coals.

DENGUE FEVER: A tropical disease caused by bites from mosquitoes carrying the dengue virus. It causes fever, headaches, muscle pain and can lead to death.

DEPOT: A place where things are stored. Explorers would often bury food for use on their return journey.

DYSENTERY: An infection which causes diarrhea. It is usually caused by poor hygiene.

ENZYMES: Proteins that speed up chemical reactions in our bodies. They help with things like breathing and digesting.

GORGE: A narrow valley with steep walls.

GOVERNOR: The British Government's representative in a colony.

GREAT ARTESIAN BASIN: An underground body of water that covers 1,700,000 square km. It lies beneath parts of the Northern Territory, Queensland, South Australia, and New South Wales.

THE GREAT AUSTRALIAN BIGHT: The large bay in the southern coast of Australia. It is 1160 km wide and is known for its rough seas.

MARINER: A sailor who assists in the navigation of a ship.

MORSE CODE: A system of dots, dashes and spaces that represent letters and can be transmitted as sounds or flashes of light.

NARDOO: A fern-like plant that is native to Australia and grows in water or mud. Aboriginal people use it as a food source, making a cake from ground up spores. If it is not prepared properly, eating it can cause death.

ORNITHOLOGIST: Someone who studies birds.

PAMPHLET: A booklet containing information or opinions about a topic, usually distributed for free.

PASTORAL LAND: Grassy land suitable for grazing cattle and sheep.

SCURVY: A disease triggered by lack of Vitamin C, resulting in sores that can cause infection.

SOUTHERN CROSS: A constellation of stars only visible in the Southern Hemisphere. It was useful when sailors were exploring the southern oceans.

SURVEYOR: Someone who surveys land. This involves measuring the exact dimensions of a piece of land.

SURVEYOR-GENERAL: A government officer who supervises surveyors. He organised expeditions into newly settled areas so that maps could be drawn. He also granted land to settlers.

TICK: Blood-sucking insect.

VITAMIN B1: A vitamin found in grains and legumes.

VITAMIN C: A vitamin found in citrus fruit and sauerkraut.

Index